BRIDGES, NOT WALLS
Building Culture Through Growth

Alejandro Gonzalez

Proof editor: Dr. Heriberto Gonzalez Valencia

ISBN: 979-8-218-84014-3

Printed in the United States of America

To my daughter Alejandra: Thank you for giving me life again. This book would not exist without the light you bring into my world. Te amo, Dios te bendiga.

Table of Contents

Preface

This book was born out of years of reflection on what truly drives growth in people and in organizations. Again and again, I found myself returning to the same simple truth: the difference between progress and decline lies in whether we build bridges or raise walls. Bridges connect. Walls divide. Bridges invite curiosity, dialogue, and trust. Walls restrict, silence, and isolate. The presence or absence of those choices explains why some cultures proper while others remain stuck.

I have seen this play out in many different settings. Sometimes it was in the manner in which a leader chose to share information openly, even when the answers were not all there. Sometimes it was in the way a team welcomed a new perspective instead of shutting it down. And sometimes it was in the way people actively listened instead of rushing to defend their own position. Each of these choices built a bridge. I have also seen the opposite: silence where there should have been honesty, defensiveness where there should have been curiosity, or exclusion where there should have been belonging. Each of those moments built a wall. Over time, those patterns define the culture, for better or for worse.

The chapters that follow are not collections of abstract theories. They are grounded in lived experiences, careful observation, and the conviction that communication, cultural diversity, leadership, and the creation of a learning culture are not optional extras. They are the core of growth itself. I did not write these pages to remain on a shelf as good intentions that never touch daily life. I wrote them to serve as reminders and challenges that can be practiced each day, no matter what the size of the organization or the scope of the team.

This book is also an invitation. It invites you to reflect on your own experiences, to see where you have already built bridges and where walls may still stand. It invites you to ask new questions about the language you use, the assumptions you carry, and the way you respond to differences. It invites you to reimagine leadership as a practice of connection rather than control, and culture as something you shape with every word and every action.

I believe that the responsibility to build bridges does not belong only to leaders at the top. It belongs to everyone. Each conversation, each decision, and each moment of listening is a chance to either strengthen connection or deepen separation. The health of a culture is not decided only in strategic planning meetings. It is decided in daily interactions, in how colleagues treat each other, and in whether people feel safe enough to bring their full selves into work.

The times we live in make this work more urgent. The world is marked by complexity, rapid change, and growing diversity. These realities can either overwhelm us or they can enrich us. The deciding factor is how we choose to respond. If we respond by building walls, we become smaller and less capable. If we respond by building bridges, we expand our capacity to learn, to adapt, and to bloom together. Growth, both personal and organizational, is not a matter of chance. It is a matter of choice.

My hope is that as you read, you will not only recognize truths that echo with your own journey but also find the courage to act on them. I hope these chapters encourage you to pause and reflect, to test your own manner of communication, and to experiment with new ways of leading and relating. More than anything, I hope this book affirms that growth never happens behind walls. It happens on the bridges we choose to create, and it continues as long as we have the courage to keep building.

Introduction

Every organization, every team, and every individual faces a constant choice: will we build bridges that connect us, or walls that divide us? This choice may not always be visible, but it is always present. It shows up in the words we use, the way we respond to one another, and the assumptions we carry into our daily interactions. Bridges invite connection, curiosity, and growth. Walls enforce silence, isolation, and limitation. Understanding this simple difference is the starting point for everything in this book.

Communication, cultural diversity, leadership, and the creation of a learning culture are not separate topics. They are pieces of the same puzzle, each incomplete without the others. Communication shapes how people comprehend one another. Diversity shapes the range of voices at the table.

Leadership shapes whether those voices are invited or silenced. And a learning culture shapes whether the organization grows from those voices or ignores them. When these elements align, bridges are built. When they are abandoned, walls appear.

Throughout the years of observing people and organizations, I have noticed how quickly culture can shift. A single leader who chooses transparency over secrecy can transform the atmosphere of an entire team. A single group that welcomes questions instead of punishing them can change the course of an organization. These shifts are not dramatic revolutions. They are simple, human choices repeated day after day. That is what makes them so powerful. They are available to everyone, at every level, at every moment.

This book reflects the belief that growth is not confined to titles or positions but is shared by every person who contributes to the culture. Growth belongs to everyone who participates in the culture. A frontline employee who speaks up with a new idea, a manager who listens with patience, a colleague who encourages a peer during a difficult moment, each of these choices creates growth. Too often we imagine leadership as something distant, reserved for the highest titles. In reality, leadership is practiced every time we decide to build a bridge.

The chapters that follow are not meant to provide quick fixes or universal formulas. Culture is too complex for that. Instead, they offer principles, perspectives, and practices that can guide reflection and action. You will find ideas about the power of language, the importance of listening, and the responsibility of leaders as teachers. You will also find reflections on how diversity becomes inclusion, how trust is built, and how learning can become a way of life rather than an occasional program. Each chapter is a piece of the larger puzzle, showing how connection creates growth.

As you read, I encourage you to move slowly. Pause at the ideas that challenge you. Reflect on the questions that rise to the surface. Consider not only what these ideas mean in theory but what they might look like in your own conversations, your own relationships, and your own work.

This book is not about information to be stored. It is about transformation that happens when ideas are put into practice.

We live in a world that needs bridges more than ever. Division, mistrust, and isolation are easy to find, not only in organizations but in communities and societies as a whole. The choice to build connection is not only a professional one. It is a human one. By choosing bridges over walls, we choose to grow together rather than apart. We choose to create cultures where people are not reduced to roles but are recognized as contributors. And we choose to believe that growth is possible, not only for organizations but for people at every stage of life.

The pages ahead will not tell you what to think. They will invite you to think differently. They will not tell you how to lead. They will encourage you to lead with connection. They will not provide walls of certainty. They will offer bridges of possibility. My hope is that by the end of this book, you will not only see the value of bridges but also find the confidence to build them wherever you are.

Chapter 1
Why Bridges, Not Walls?

Human development has always been shaped by the presence of bridges and walls. Both are built with purpose, and both carry meaning that extends beyond stone, steel, or wood. A bridge is never just a structure; it is an act of intention, a decision to gauge a distance and create connection. A wall is never only a barrier; it is a choice to protect, but also to separate and isolate. These metaphors live not only in our cities but also in our conversations, relationships, and organizations.

Think about the last time you felt truly connected to a person, a team, or a workplace. Chances are, someone built a bridge, perhaps through a kind word, a clear explanation, or a willingness to listen. Now think about the last time you felt excluded, dismissed, or left in the dark. Somewhere in that moment, a wall was raised. These choices are rarely dramatic. They are made quietly, in everyday language, in subtle decisions, and in how people show up for one another. Yet over time they define the culture.

A bridge does not erase distance. It acknowledges difference and creates a way across. The very existence of a bridge implies that separation was there first, whether physical, emotional, or cultural. In organizations, those separations can take the form of title, role, background, or perspective. When bridges are built, those differences remain, but they are no longer obstacles. They become opportunities for exchange. A wall, in contrast, often provides a false sense of safety. It may feel protective at first, but it isolates. What seems secure eventually becomes confining.

Walls in organizations often appear in subtle ways. Leaders may withhold information in the name of control. Teams may guard their expertise to protect their value. Employees may remain silent, convinced that speaking up will only invite criticism. These walls are rarely intentional, but they are powerful. They limit trust, reduce creativity, and prevent people from seeing beyond their own viewpoint. Bridges, on the other hand, open space for dialogue. They allow knowledge to flow, ideas to cross boundaries, and people to move toward one another with greater understanding.

Consider communication. A leader who shares openly, even when answers are incomplete, builds a bridge. That honesty invites trust. A leader who avoids difficult conversations builds a wall, even if unintentionally. Employees may feel protected from uncomfortable truths for a moment, but soon they begin to wonder what else is being kept from them. Over time, silence erodes confidence faster than imperfect honesty ever could.

Think also about collaboration. A team that invites diverse perspectives, even if it slows the process, is building bridges. Each contribution stretches the group's vision further. A team that shuts down input in the name of efficiency is building walls. The work may move quickly in the short term, but innovation condenses. The bridge invites growth: the wall limits it.

This metaphor is not simply poetic. It is practical. Every organization faces challenges: competition, limited resources, shifting demands, and unexpected crises. How people respond to these challenges depends on whether their culture is built on bridges or walls. Cultures built on walls tend to react with defensiveness. They protect what they already know and close themselves off to possibility. Cultures built on bridges respond with openness. They learn, they adapt, and they grow stronger precisely because they stay connected.

When I speak of bridges, I do not mean blind optimism. Building a bridge does not mean ignoring real risks or differences. It means choosing connection over separation, transparency over secrecy, and trust over suspicion. A bridge acknowledges the gap and dares to cross it. A wall acknowledges the gap and chooses to deepen it. One leads to growth, the other leads to a downswing.

I have seen both in action. There are times when leaders built walls out of fear, hiding behind authority rather than engaging with their teams. In those moments, talent was wasted because people did not feel trusted to contribute. I have also seen the power of bridges, when leaders admitted what they did not know, asked for input, and created space for honest conversation. Those moments did more to build loyalty and creativity than any incentive program ever could.

The lesson is simple: growth never happens behind walls. Walls may delay mistakes, but they also prevent progress. Bridges carry risk, to cross is to be vulnerable, but they also carry reward. They create movement, and growth is always movement.

So, what does this look like in everyday work? It might mean choosing to give feedback directly rather than avoiding it. It might mean inviting someone from outside your usual circle into a conversation, knowing their perspective could stretch your thinking. It might mean admitting uncertainty rather than pretending to have all the answers. These are small acts of bridge-building but repeated over time they transform the culture.

A practical exercise is to ask yourself at the end of each week: Did I build more bridges or walls this week? Think of one moment where you chose connection and one moment where you may have chosen separation. This simple reflection makes the metaphor real. Over time, it will also reveal patterns. Some people and situations naturally invite bridges; others trigger walls. Awareness is the first step toward change.

This book is not about tearing down every wall recklessly. Some walls are necessary: compliance, safety, and structure matter. But the danger comes when walls become the default, when they are built not to protect but to avoid. The challenge of leadership, communication, and culture is to know where a wall is essential and where a bridge is possible.

As you move into the next chapters, keep the image of bridges and walls close. Every decision at its core, a choice between the two. One path limits. The other expands. Bridges, not walls, are where growth begins.

Chapter 2
The Language of Growth

Language is the most powerful tool within any organization. It shapes how people perceive reality, how they interpret one another's intentions, and how they decide whether to contribute or to retreat. A single phrase can open a door, while another can quietly close it. When we speak of building bridges rather than walls, much of that work begins with words. Language is where trust is either created or destroyed, where belonging is either confirmed or denied, and where growth is either invited or shut down.

Think about how a simple sentence can change the direction of a conversation. When a manager says, "*That idea will never work,*" a wall is raised. The person who offered the idea now has to decide whether to stay quiet in the future. Contrast that with the words, "*Tell me more about how that could work.*" Even if the idea is not perfect, the bridge has been built. The language shifts from judgment to curiosity, from finality to possibility. The difference is only a few words, but the impact is profound.

The language of growth is not about polished speeches or motivational slogans. It is not what is printed on posters or in company handbooks. It is the everyday language of meetings, check-ins, feedback sessions, and hallway conversations. Culture does not live in what leaders declare during large gatherings. It lives in what people say to one another when no one is watching. When language is filled with respect, curiosity, and clarity, people feel encouraged to contribute. When it is filled with dismissal, vagueness, or sarcasm, people retreat behind walls of silence.

One of the most damaging patterns in organizations is the use of language that confuses rather than clarifies. When leaders speak in abstractions that sound polished but say little, employees may nod along but leave with uncertainty.

Confusion builds walls because people do not want to admit they do not understand. Clarity builds bridges. When leaders explain with simplicity, even complex ideas become accessible. People feel safe to ask questions, and questions themselves become valued. Clarity is an act of respect because it communicates that everyone deserves to understand.

Listening is just as much a part of the language of growth as speaking. Too often, listening is treated as the pause between responses rather than an intentional act of engagement. True listening signals that the words of others matter. When someone feels heard, they feel connected. When someone feels ignored, they feel isolated. Listening is not passive. It is an active form of communication that can either build a bridge or reinforce a wall.

Silence itself can carry meaning. In some cases, silence shows reflection and respect. In others, it communicates fear or disapproval. Leaders must pay attention not only to what is said but also to what is left unsaid. If meetings are consistently dominated by a few voices while others remain quiet, it is worth asking whether those silences are signs of agreement or signs of walls being built. When silence comes from fear, bridges must be built through invitation. A simple "*I would like to hear your perspective*" can turn absence into connection.

The language of growth is also shaped by how feedback is delivered. Feedback can be one of the strongest tools for development, but only if it is given in a way that encourages rather than crushes. Consider the difference between "*You need to fix this*" and "*Here is something you can try differently next time.*" The first isolates the person from their potential, while the second links them to a path forward. Walls are built when feedback humiliates or shuts down possibility. Bridges are built when feedback is framed as part of a journey of improvement.

Language reflects the values of the culture. If leaders use language that constantly emphasizes competition and scarcity, employees may adopt a defensive mindset. If leaders use language that highlights collaboration, trust, and growth, employees will lean toward those same values. Over time, words create habits, and habits create culture. This is why small changes in language matter. They ripple out and downward, influencing how people behave and how they see their roles within the larger whole.

To bring this idea into daily work, consider practicing intentional shifts in language. Replace judgment with curiosity. Instead of saying *"That is wrong,"* try *"How else might we see this?"* Replace finality with openness. Instead of *"This is how we have always done it,"* try *"Is there a better way to do this now?"* Replace dismissal with recognition. Instead of *"We do not have time for that,"* try *"That is worth noting, let us capture it for later."* These subtle shifts build bridges without requiring dramatic changes in process.

Another practical exercise is to reflect on your own phrases. At the end of a meeting, ask yourself: Did my words build bridges or walls? Were people more open and engaged when the conversation ended than when it began, or less so? Reflection creates awareness, and awareness creates change. Over time, this habit transforms language from something automatic into something intentional.

Every conversation is a chance to choose. Language can reduce someone to silence, or it can elevate their confidence. It can guard information, or it can share it freely. It can reinforce the status quo, or it can spark new possibilities. The choice may seem small in the moment, but the cumulative effect of language shapes entire cultures.

Bridges are not built with bricks alone. They are built with words. And words chosen with care, respect, and clarity will always carry people further than walls of silence or judgment ever could. The language of growth is the language of connection, and it is the language of cultures where growth never stops.

Chapter 3

Culture Shapes Conversation

Every conversation that happens in an organization is influenced by culture. Culture is not something abstract that lives on a wall in the form of values written for display. It is something that shows up in tone, in rhythm, and in the way, people interpret one another's words. Two people can say the same phrase in different cultures and the meaning can be completely different. A pause can be seen as respect in one context and as disagreement in another. Directness can be celebrated as honesty in one culture and criticized as rudeness in another. These subtle differences shape not only how conversations unfold but also how trust is built.

When organizations overlook the role of culture in communication, misunderstandings grow. A leader may believe they are being clear, but their message is filtered through assumptions that come from their own background and habits. Employees may remain silent, not because they lack ideas, but because their culture discourages direct disagreement. Others may speak up quickly, convinced that contribution is valued only if it is immediate and confident. Without awareness, these differences create walls. With awareness, they create depth which in turn become bridges.

Culture provides more than context. It provides strength. Some traditions emphasize precision and discipline, others creativity and experimentation, and others collaboration and harmony. None of these strengths is complete by itself. But when combined, they allow an organization to see more broadly and respond more effectively. A team that values discipline learns from a team that values creativity. A team that values speed learns from a team that values reflection. When cultures share and learn from one another, the result is resilience.

This kind of learning does not happen on its own. It requires humility. Leaders and employees alike must be willing to recognize that their way is not the only way. For example, a manager who values fast decision-making may become impatient with an employee who prefers careful consideration. Instead of labeling the difference as a weakness, the manager can choose to see it as balance. The conversation shifts from frustration to opportunity. Bridges are built when differences are acknowledged with curiosity rather than resisted with judgment.

These ideas are not only about nationality or ethnicity. Culture exists within departments, professions, and even generations. The language of an engineering team may be filled with technical precision. The language of a marketing team may be filled with metaphor and storytelling. Both can learn from each other, but only if they are willing to build bridges. Generational culture adds another layer. Younger employees may expect frequent feedback and digital communication, while older employees may value face-to-face dialogue and independent work. Neither approach is wrong. Both carry wisdom. Culture becomes a wall when these differences are seen as threats, but it becomes a bridge when they are seen as gifts.

The work of leaders and employees is to create spaces where these cultural differences can coexist without silencing one another. This requires intentional conversation. It may mean asking a quieter employee for their perspective rather than assuming silence means agreement. It may mean pausing to reflect on whether a sharp disagreement is rooted in ideas or in cultural style. It may mean slowing down a fast-paced discussion to ensure that careful thinkers have time to contribute. These choices signal that culture is not something to overcome but something to respect.

Practical reflection helps to make this real. At the end of a meeting, ask whether every voice was heard or whether the loudest voices dominated. Think about whether silence came from reflection or from hesitation. Consider whether the conversation reflected a balance of perspectives or leaned heavily toward one style. These reflections reveal whether culture is acting as a bridge or as a wall. They also create opportunities to make small adjustments that have lasting effects.

Culture is present whether we acknowledge it or not. It does not disappear simply because an organization chooses not to talk about it. The choice is whether culture will be allowed to separate or to connect. Organizations that treat culture as a wall close themselves off to growth. Those that treat it as a bridge gain the ability to learn from differences, to adapt more quickly, and to expand their capacity.

At its heart, culture shapes conversation. Conversation shapes relationships. And relationships shape results. If the culture invites openness, curiosity, and respect, the conversations will carry those qualities forward. If the culture rewards defensiveness, conformity, or silence, the conversations will carry those as well. The bridge is not automatic. It is built every time people choose to recognize cultural differences as opportunities rather than obstacles.

Growth begins when organizations stop asking how to eliminate differences and start asking how to connect across them. Bridges of culture are built when people see that another way of communicating is not a threat but a window. The strongest conversations happen when many perspectives meet. And it is in those conversations, shaped by culture and guided by connection, that organizations find their path to growth that never stops.

Bridges built through culture are not one-time efforts. They must be maintained with patience, intentionality, and the willingness to learn continuously. Each conversation becomes either a small repair that strengthens the structure or a small crack that weakens it. When leaders and teams understand this, they treat every interaction as meaningful. Culture is not only what we inherit but what we choose to build, one bridge at a time.

Chapter 4

From Diversity to Inclusion

Diversity is often celebrated as a goal, yet on its own it is only the beginning. Having people from different backgrounds, experiences, and perspectives in the same room does not automatically lead to better conversations, stronger decisions, or deeper trust. Diversity simply counts who is present. Inclusion determines who participates. The difference between the two is the difference between potential and reality.

An organization may be diverse in numbers but motionless in practice. This happens when certain voices dominate while others remain unheard, or when people are physically present but emotionally absent. A workplace can gather people of different genders, cultures, and ages, yet if only a select few are truly influencing decisions, then diversity is little more than a statistic. Inclusion takes the next step. It ensures that people are not only at the table but are also invited to speak, encouraged to share, and taken seriously when they do.

Inclusion transforms diversity into strength. When people see that their contributions matter, they are more likely to offer ideas, to take risks, and to engage fully. They no longer carry the burden of proving they belong. Instead, they experience belonging as a given. This sense of belonging shifts the culture from guarded to generous. People stop holding back and start leaning in, and the collective capacity of the organization expands.

The path to inclusion requires courage. Conversations about bias, equity, and privilege are not easy. They may cause discomfort because they ask people to examine assumptions that have gone unchallenged for years. Avoiding these conversations may feel safer, but it builds walls of silence that weaken trust. Facing them with honesty and respect builds bridges that strengthen them. The very act of acknowledging that inclusion is not automatic is a step toward growth.

Consider how decisions are made. In some organizations, leadership teams reflect diversity, but the voices that carry weight remain predictable. Decisions may be presented as collaborative when in truth they reflect only a narrow slice of perspectives. Employees recognize this quickly. They see that diversity has not translated into influence. Inclusion, on the other hand, makes influence visible. It shows up in whose ideas are implemented, whose concerns are addressed, and whose input shapes the future.

The difference becomes clear in meetings. Imagine a room where several people hesitate to speak because their ideas have been dismissed before. The diversity is there, but it is silent. Now imagine a room where those same individuals are asked directly for their thoughts, where their ideas are acknowledged, and where their input helps guide the decision. The shift may seem small in the moment, but over time it rewires the culture. Walls of exclusion are replaced by bridges of participation.

Inclusion does not mean agreement on everything. It means respect for every voice. An inclusive culture welcomes disagreement because it understands that different perspectives sharpen ideas. Where walls exist, disagreement is seen as threat. Where bridges exist, disagreement is seen as opportunity. When handled with respect, disagreement leads to better outcomes because it forces teams to test assumptions and refine decisions. Inclusion makes that process possible.

The movement from diversity to inclusion is also about power. Too often, diversity initiatives stop at representation, as though presence alone is enough. True inclusion asks harder questions: Who sets the agenda? Who decides the priorities? Who benefits from the outcomes? Inclusion ensures that power is shared rather than concentrated, and that opportunities for growth are distributed fairly. Without this shift, diversity remains surface level. With it, diversity becomes a catalyst for transformation.

Practical reflection can help bring these ideas into daily life. After a meeting, ask whether the conversation was shaped by a variety of voices or whether the same people carried the weight. Pay attention to who speaks freely and who seems hesitant. Ask whether contributions from different perspectives are recognized equally, or whether some are overlooked. These questions reveal whether the culture is moving toward bridges of inclusion or walls of exclusion.

Inclusion is not a final destination but an ongoing practice. Cultures change over time, and what feels inclusive today may not be enough tomorrow. The key is to remain attentive, to listen deeply, and to adapt continually. Inclusion lives in habits, not in declarations. It is demonstrated in how people are treated, how decisions are made, and how respect is shown in the details of daily work.

When diversity is present but inclusion is absent, growth remains stalled. When inclusion takes root, diversity becomes a living strength. People no longer wonder whether their presence matters. They know it does because they see the evidence in the culture around them. Walls of silence and hesitation fall, and bridges of trust and belonging rise.

Inclusion ensures that diversity is not an image but a reality. It makes difference not something to be tolerated but something to be valued. It turns potential into participation, presence into influence, and statistics into stories of growth. And when inclusion becomes part of the culture, diversity is no longer fragile. It is strong, resilient, and alive.

Chapter 5

Breaking Barriers, Building Trust

Trust is the foundation of every relationship, whether personal or professional. Without it, even the most talented groups struggle to collaborate. With it, ordinary people accomplish extraordinary things. In organizations, trust is both delicate and essential. It is fragile because it depends on consistency, honesty, and respect, and even small breaks can weaken it. Yet it is essential because without trust, communication falters, collaboration diminishes, and growth slows.

Barriers to trust appear in many forms. They are often subtle, laced into the daily habits of the workplace. A leader who promises more than they deliver creates a small crack in trust. An employee who withholds concerns out of fear adds another. Over time, these small cracks form walls. The result is a culture where people guard themselves rather than engage openly. They speak cautiously, share less, and retreat behind silence. These behaviors are not signs of laziness or disengagement. They are signs that trust has been damaged.

Breaking barriers begins with recognition. Leaders must be willing to acknowledge that walls exist. Pretending that everyone feels safe and respected does not create safety. It hides the problem and allows it to deepen. Trust grows when people admit the truth about where barriers stand. This admission may feel uncomfortable, but it is the first step toward repair.

Consistency is one of the strongest tools for building trust. Words must align with actions. Promises must be kept, not occasionally but regularly. Employees quickly notice whether their leaders can be relied upon. They pay attention to whether standards are applied fairly, whether feedback is delivered respectfully, and whether recognition is given genuinely. Inconsistent behavior builds walls faster than any policy. Consistent behavior builds bridges, even if progress is slow.

Vulnerability also builds trust. Leaders who admit mistakes, seek feedback, or share challenges signal that openness is safe. Employees respond with openness of their own. This does not weaken authority. It strengthens it, because people prefer to follow leaders who are human rather than leaders who pretend to be perfect. Vulnerability invites harmony. When one person chooses to be genuine, others follow. Over time, the culture shifts, and authenticity becomes valued more than appearances.

Trust in diverse environments requires more than familiarity. It requires respect for difference. People must believe not only that they are accepted but also that their perspectives contribute meaningfully. A workplace that welcomes many backgrounds but ignores their input is not truly inclusive. Trust is only complete when diversity and inclusion are accompanied by influence. Belonging occurs when individuals see their ideas taken seriously, their contributions implemented, and their identities respected.

Conflict is often misunderstood as a threat to trust. In truth, conflict handled with respect strengthens it. Avoiding conflict may feel safe, but it builds walls of resentment. Addressing conflict openly, listening carefully, and seeking fair solutions builds bridges. People learn that they can disagree without being excluded. They discover that their voice matters even when it challenges others. Conflict becomes an opportunity to deepen trust rather than to damage it.

Leaders play a central role in breaking barriers. Their behavior sets the standard for everyone else. If leaders respond to mistakes with punishment, employees learn to hide errors. If leaders respond with curiosity, employees learn to share openly. If leaders prioritize transparency, employees follow suit. If leaders create secrecy, employees guard themselves. Every choice either strengthens a bridge or raises a wall. Leadership is never neutral in matters of trust.

Practical reflection can reveal where barriers still exist. Ask whether employees feel free to speak honestly. Notice whether new ideas are welcomed or dismissed. Pay attention to whether recognition is spread widely or concentrated among a few. These questions reveal whether trust is growing or shrinking. They also provide opportunities to act. Each adjustment, however small, is a chance to lower a wall and build a bridge.

The power of trust is that it multiplies. When one bridge is built, others follow. People who feel trusted extend trust to others. Teams that experience honesty become more willing to share honestly themselves. Trust is contagious. So is the absence of it. A culture built on walls of suspicion spreads just as quickly, but it spreads in the opposite direction. Leaders and employees alike must decide which they want to multiply.

Breaking barriers and building trust is not a single achievement. It is an ongoing practice. Walls may appear again, because disappointment, mistakes, and misunderstandings are inevitable. What matters is the response. When people are committed to repair, trust can survive failure. When people are unwilling to face the damage, walls grow higher. The difference is not perfection but persistence.

Trust is what allows communication to flourish, diversity to become strength, and inclusion to move from aspiration to reality. Without it, progress is fragile. With it, barriers become temporary, and bridges multiply. Trust turns connection into resilience and transforms growth into something that lasts.

Chapter 6

The Leader's Role in Connection

Leadership is more than a title or a position of authority. It is the daily practice of shaping the environment in which people work, grow, and relate to one another. Leaders may carry responsibility for goals and results, but their greatest influence lies in how they connect with people. Every word, every choice, and even every silence communicates something about the culture. A leader may believe that by saying nothing they are being neutral, but silence also carries meaning. Leadership is never neutral. It either builds bridges or raises walls.

Connection is at the heart of effective leadership. This does not mean that a leader must be liked by everyone or must avoid conflict. Connection means being present, consistent, and trustworthy. Employees do not expect perfection, but they do expect honesty. When leaders communicate clearly, listen carefully, and follow through on their commitments, they create a climate of safety. In that climate, people are willing to contribute, take risks, and admit mistakes. Without it, they retreat behind caution and silence, unsure whether they can trust their voices will matter.

The voice of a leader carries particular weight because it sets the tone for everyone else. A casual comment from a supervisor can either encourage initiative or silence it. A manager's willingness to listen can either invite dialogue or close it off. Employees hear not only the content of a leader's words but also the values behind them. Respect, fairness, and belonging are communicated not through slogans but through the way leaders respond in everyday moments. A single sentence can be a bridge that draws people in or a wall that pushes them away.

Modeling matters. Leaders set examples that are often imitated without question. A leader who listens with patience shows that listening is valued, and employees copy that habit. A leader who dismisses ideas quickly shows that dismissiveness is acceptable, and employees copy that as well. Culture is not shaped primarily by declarations. It is shaped by repetition. Day after day, leaders demonstrate whether connection is a priority or an afterthought, and employees follow the example.

Connection becomes even more important in moments of uncertainty. Change, disruption, or crisis can unsettle people. In those times, employees look to leaders for stability. If leaders build bridges by acknowledging concerns, explaining decisions, and inviting input, they guide their teams across uncertainty with trust intact. If they raise walls by withholding information or avoiding dialogue, they deepen anxiety and erode confidence. Crisis does not create leadership qualities. It reveals them.

Connection also means recognizing difference. In diverse organizations, leaders must adapt their style to connect across cultures, generations, and backgrounds. What motivates one employee may discourage another. What feels respectful to one group may feel distant to another. A leader who insists on treating everyone exactly the same may believe they are being fair, but fairness does not always mean sameness. Connection requires attentiveness to what makes each individual unique. It requires a leader to meet people where they are while staying authentic to their own values.

Practical connection often looks simple, but its impact is deep. It may be as basic as remembering names, acknowledging effort, or making time for one-on-one conversations. It may mean asking open questions rather than giving quick answers. It may mean following up on concerns instead of letting them fade. These actions show that people are seen and valued. When repeated consistently, they build trust that becomes the foundation of growth.

The leader's role in connection is also about creating bridges between people, not only between leader and employee. Leaders who encourage collaboration across teams, departments, or perspectives demonstrate that growth happens collectively. They do not place themselves at the center of every interaction but act as facilitators who make connections possible. In doing so, they multiply the number of bridges in the culture, ensuring that trust and communication flow beyond their own relationships.

Ultimately, the leader's role is not to stand above others but to stand among them as a connector. A leader builds the first bridge by extending trust, opening dialogue, and demonstrating respect. Once that bridge is in place, others begin to build their own. Over time, the culture shifts, and walls lose their power. Leaders who understand this leave behind more than results. They leave behind a network of bridges that continue to support growth long after their own presence has moved on.

Chapter 7
Leading Across Cultures

Leadership in today's world is no longer limited by geography. Teams often include people from different countries, backgrounds, and traditions, and even when they share a physical space, they bring with them cultural perspectives shaped by family, education, and community. To lead across cultures is not only a professional skill but also a human responsibility. It is about recognizing that differences are not obstacles to overcome but resources to learn from. The leader's task is to turn those differences into strengths by building bridges of understanding and respect.

Cultural differences show up in the smallest details of communication. What seems polite in one culture may feel distant in another. A leader who prizes directness may unintentionally appear harsh to someone who values diplomacy. An employee who pauses to reflect before speaking may be misjudged as hesitant by someone who values quick responses. None of these differences are signs of weakness. They are signs of distinct ways of making meaning. Leaders who fail to recognize them often build walls of misunderstanding. Leaders who pay attention and adapt build bridges of trust.

Respect is the foundation of cross-cultural leadership. Respect does not mean ignoring differences. It means acknowledging them openly and treating them as worthy of attention. For example, a leader who notices that some employees remain quiet in meetings can take time to invite their input in ways that feel safe. They might provide questions in advance, allow for written responses, or check in privately afterward. These small adjustments communicate that every perspective is valued, regardless of communication style. Over time, respect turns difference into belonging.

Curiosity is another essential quality. Too often, cultural differences are treated as problems to solve rather than as opportunities to explore. A curious leader asks, *"What can I learn from this perspective?"* instead of *"How do I get them to adapt to mine?"* Curiosity lowers defenses and opens the door to deeper understanding. When leaders model curiosity, they encourage their teams to adopt the same approach. Conversations shift from confrontation to exploration, and bridges form naturally.

Leading across cultures also requires awareness of power dynamics. People from underrepresented backgrounds may hesitate to challenge authority, fearing their voice will not be respected. Leaders must recognize this and create spaces where speaking up is encouraged and protected. This might involve setting clear expectations that disagreement is not only acceptable but also valuable. It might involve expanding contributions that might otherwise be overlooked. Inclusion does not happen by accident. It happens when leaders intentionally distribute influence across all voices.

Trust is particularly fragile in cross-cultural contexts. Misunderstandings can happen easily, and if left ignored, they can grow into patterns of doubt that separate people. Leaders must learn to clarify intentions and to check for understanding. A simple question such as *"How did you hear what I just said?"* can reveal whether a message landed as intended. By slowing down to make sure everyone is on the same page, small misunderstandings are stopped before they grow bigger. It also communicates humility, a quality that strengthens trust across every culture.

Practical leadership across cultures means creating rituals and habits that reinforce connection. This might include celebrating a variety of cultural holidays, incorporating diverse perspectives into decision-making, or encouraging employees to share elements of their background that shape how they work. These practices do more than acknowledge differences. They invite people to bring their whole selves into the workplace. When people no longer feel they must hide who they are, their energy shifts from self-protection to contribution.

Leaders also need to be mindful of their own biases. Everyone carries assumptions shaped by their upbringing, and these assumptions can limit how they interpret others. Effective leaders do not pretend to be free of bias. They acknowledge it, examine it, and work to reduce its impact. Self-awareness is the first step toward fairness. By recognizing their own blind spots, leaders set an example that it is acceptable, and even necessary, to reflect and to grow.

The reward of leading across cultures is a stronger, more innovative organization. Diverse perspectives generate ideas that no single viewpoint could produce alone. Different ways of problem-solving reveal alternatives that might otherwise remain hidden. Conflict, when approached with respect, sparks creativity instead of division. In this sense, culture is not a barrier to overcome but a resource to multiply. Leaders who see it this way unlock the full potential of their teams.

Ultimately, leading across cultures is about building bridges that carry people toward shared goals without erasing the uniqueness of their identities. It is about creating a space where difference is not feared but valued, where communication flows despite variation, and where trust holds strong even in the presence of tension. Leaders who succeed in this role leave behind organizations that are not only effective but also people-centered. They prove that when bridges are built across cultures, growth does not just continue. It expands.

Leading across cultures is not a skill that is mastered once and then complete. It is a lifelong practice of humility, openness, and learning. Each new person, each new team, and each new challenge presents an opportunity to see the world through another lens. Leaders who approach this practice with consistency discover that cultural differences are not sources of division but sources of strength. Ultimately, the bridges they build across cultures become the strongest foundations of lasting growth.

Chapter 8
Growth Through People

Active listening is one of the simplest acts a leader can perform, yet it is also one of the most powerful. Too often it is mistaken for silence, as if active listening means simply waiting until it is one's turn to speak. True active listening is far more than that. It requires attention, presence, and a willingness to set aside assumptions. Active listening is not only about hearing words but also about understanding meaning, emotion, and intention. When practiced well, it becomes a bridge that connects people across distance and difference.

Many organizations underestimate the role of active listening in shaping culture. They create strategies for communication that focus on what leaders will say and how messages will be delivered, yet they neglect to ask how those messages will be received. When people feel that their voices are not heard, they begin to withdraw. They may still show up physically, but their energy and commitment start to fade, referred to as quiet quitting. Over time, the silence that results from poor listening is more damaging than any single mistake. A culture that actively listens grows stronger; a culture that does not listen builds walls of indifference.

Active listening is an expression of respect. It signals that the other person's perspective has value. When leaders actively listen, employees feel acknowledged, even if their ideas are not adopted. The act of active listening itself communicates belonging. In contrast, when leaders appear distracted, interrupt frequently, or rush to respond, they send a message that the other person's voice does not matter. The difference between connection and exclusion is often measured not by what leaders say but by how they listen.

Effective active listening requires more than patience. It requires curiosity. Curiosity transforms listening from a duty into a practice of discovery. A curious listener does not simply wait for the other person to finish but asks questions that go deeper. They want to know what lies beneath the words, what experiences shaped the perspective, and what possibilities might be uncovered through dialogue. This type of listening builds bridges because it creates space for mutual learning rather than one-way communication.

Active listening is also about presence. In a world filled with distraction, presence is rare and therefore powerful. Leaders who put away their phones, close their laptops, and give full attention to the speaker create an environment of respect. The message is clear: this conversation matters, and you matter. Presence cannot be faked. People can tell when attention is divided, and they can also tell when it is genuine. The quality of connection rises in proportion to the quality of presence.

The power of listening extends to conflict. Many conflicts escalate not because of the issues themselves but because people feel unheard. When each side focuses only on defending their position, walls rise quickly. But when one side chooses to actively listen, the tone shifts. The act of hearing the other person's perspective does not erase disagreement, but it softens defensiveness and makes resolution possible. In this way, listening is not weakness. It is strength, because it creates the conditions for trust even amid tension.

Active listening also serves as a tool for innovation. New ideas rarely emerge fully formed. They grow through conversation, refinement, and feedback. Leaders who actively listen catch insights that might otherwise be overlooked. They recognize patterns across different voices, connecting fragments into larger possibilities. Innovation requires more than creativity; it requires receptivity. A culture that values listening multiplies its chances of discovering something new.

To make active listening part of daily practice, leaders must slow down. Too often, the pace of work rewards quick decisions and fast responses. While speed has its place, depth requires time. Active listening cannot be rushed. It takes patience to let someone finish a thought, to ask clarifying questions, and to sit with answers that may be incomplete. Leaders who consistently make time for actively listening send a powerful message about priorities. They demonstrate that people matter as much as results, and that relationships matter as much as outcomes.

There is also a personal dimension to listening. Each of us carries assumptions that shape how we interpret others. True active listening requires awareness of those assumptions. It asks us to notice when we are filtering words through our own biases and to be willing to set those biases aside. This kind of listening is not easy, but it is transformative. It allows us to hear not only what others say but also who they are. In doing so, it creates connection at a level deeper than words.

The power of actively listening lies in its simplicity. It does not require advanced skills or elaborate training. It requires willingness. Anyone can choose to listen more carefully, more openly, and more often. The impact of that choice is profound. It builds trust, reduces conflict, and strengthens culture. It reminds people that their voice matters, and when people believe that they contribute with energy and confidence. Listening becomes more than a tool. It becomes a way of leading, a way of building bridges where growth never stops.

Listening also has a collective dimension. When entire teams practice active listening, the culture changes. Meetings shift from contests of who can speak the loudest to shared spaces where ideas are explored thoughtfully. Teams that listen to one another learn to anticipate needs, to support different working styles, and to build trust more quickly. The energy of the group moves from competition toward collaboration, and in that shift, performance rises naturally.

Listening has the power to heal. Many workplaces carry histories of mistrust, disappointment, or neglect. People remember the times when their voices were ignored, and those memories create invisible walls that linger. Leaders who choose to listen with patience and empathy can begin to repair that damage.

Chapter 9
Defining a Learning Culture

At the center of leadership lies communication. It is not a skill to be added once other tasks are mastered. Communication is the very core of what it means to lead. Without it, vision remains hidden, values remain abstract, and direction remains unclear. With it, people know where they are going, why it matters, and how they can contribute. Leadership begins and ends with the ability to connect through words and presence.

Some leaders mistake communication for performance. They believe that as long as they can deliver a strong speech or a polished presentation, they have fulfilled their responsibility. But communication is far more than a moment on a stage. It lives in daily interactions, in hallway conversations, in emails, and in the way, leaders respond to sudden, out-of-the-blue questions. These smaller moments often carry more influence than the formal ones, because they reveal authenticity. Employees remember not only what a leader says during official meetings but also how they speak in casual exchanges.

Communication is not only about clarity of message. It is about alignment between message and action. When words do not match behavior, trust fades. Leaders who speak of respect but act dismissively build walls. Leaders who promise transparency but hide key information create suspicion. Alignment is what makes communication credible. Without it, even eloquent words lose power. With it, even simple words carry weight.

The best leaders communicate with a sense of presence. Presence means being fully engaged in the moment rather than distracted or rushed. When leaders speak with presence, people feel that their attention is undivided. When leaders listen with presence, people feel that their voice matters.

Presence is a bridge that cannot be faked. People sense it immediately, and it is remembered long after the details of the conversation fade.

One of the most overlooked aspects of leadership communication is consistency. Messages that are delivered once and never repeated rarely take hold. People need reinforcement, not because they are incapable of remembering but because reinforcement signals commitment. When a leader communicates values repeatedly, in different contexts and through different examples, those values become part of the fabric of the culture. Consistency builds reliability. Inconsistent messages, on the other hand, create confusion and weaken trust.

Communication is the doorway leaders use to invite others into ownership. When leaders speak in ways that clarify roles, acknowledge contributions, and explain purpose, people feel connected to the larger mission. They see themselves not only as employees but as partners in progress. A workplace where communication flows openly becomes a place where people invest their energy freely. They no longer feel that they are simply following instructions. They feel that they are part of something meaningful.

In times of change or uncertainty, communication becomes even more critical. Silence leaves room for fear, speculation, and rumor. Clear and timely communication, even if incomplete, creates stability. Employees would rather hear that a decision is still being shaped than hear nothing at all. The absence of communication is in itself a form of communication, and it rarely builds trust. Leaders who understand this choose to speak honestly, even when the answers are not yet final.

Authenticity is the final measure of communication. Employees quickly recognize when words are rehearsed but not lived. Authentic communication does not require perfection. It requires sincerity. Leaders who admit challenges, acknowledge mistakes, and share real experiences connect more deeply than those who try to appear flawless. Authentic words reach beyond the surface and touch the core of human connection. They remind people that leadership is not about distance but about relationship.

At its core, leadership is communication. Every plan, every strategy, and every initiative depends on how well it is communicated. If the words are unclear, the actions will be scattered. If the words are inconsistent, the trust will be weak. But if the words are aligned, consistent, and authentic, the team and thus the organization will move forward with energy. Communication is not one part of leadership. It is the center from which everything else grows.

Leaders who build bridges do not stop at vision; they translate vision into concrete steps. One of the most effective ways to do this is through SMART Goals: Specific, Measurable, Achievable, Relevant, and Time-bound. This approach keeps growth from remaining abstract and ensures that progress can be tracked, celebrated, and sustained. The real question for every leader is not whether goals are set, but whether they are set in a way that inspires people to truly grow.

Chapter 10

The Four Pillars in Action

Leadership is often imagined as a destination, a point at which a person has arrived and earned the right to guide others. In truth, leadership is less about arrival and more about continuation. It is not a place of certainty but a place of constant learning. The most effective leaders are not those who know everything but those who never stop growing. They understand that their ability to lead others depends on their willingness to learn themselves.

Learning as a leader requires humility. To admit that there is more to discover is to accept vulnerability, and many avoid it because it feels risky. Yet this humility is what gives leaders credibility. People trust leaders who show they do not have all the answers but remain committed to learning. They respect those who seek knowledge rather than pretend to already possess it. Humility does not weaken authority. It strengthens it, because it signals honesty. People would rather follow someone who grows openly than someone who hides behind an image of perfection.

Leaders who embrace learning set the tone for their organizations. When they engage in professional development, seek feedback, or invite new ideas, they model a culture of growth. Their behavior gives permission for others to do the same. In workplaces where leaders are rigid, employees often hesitate to experiment, fearing mistakes will be punished. In workplaces where leaders show curiosity and openness, employees follow with innovation and energy. Learning at the top opens space for learning everywhere else.

The responsibility of learning also includes reflection. Leaders must examine new information and their own experiences. Reflection turns events into lessons. A success can reveal what worked well and should be repeated. A failure can reveal what needs to change. Without reflection, experiences pass by without meaning. With reflection, even challenges become sources of growth. Leaders who pause and make thoughtful adjustments show that meaningful learning values depth over speed.

Learning also requires seeking diverse perspectives. No single leader, no matter how experienced, can see every angle of a situation. By inviting input from others, leaders expand their vision. This is especially important in diverse environments where people bring different cultural, professional, and personal insights. A leader who welcomes these voices learns more than they could alone. They also build bridges of inclusion, showing that wisdom is not concentrated in one person but distributed throughout the group.

The responsibility to learn extends to change. The world shifts quickly, and leadership that was effective yesterday may not be enough tomorrow. Leaders must adapt, whether through new technologies, changing markets, or evolving expectations. Resistance to change builds walls that isolate organizations from progress. Openness to change builds bridges that carry them into the future. The leader's role is to guide others through change, and that guidance is only credible when the leader themselves is willing to learn.

Practical steps for leaders include seeking mentors, reading, participating in training, and engaging in dialogue with peers both within their organization and in other industries. But learning also comes from actively listening to employees, paying attention to feedback, and being willing to reconsider long-held assumptions. A leader who limits learning to formal programs misses the lessons present in daily interactions. Every conversation holds the possibility of discovery. Every challenge holds the possibility of growth.

When leaders neglect learning, they stall, and so does their organization. They may rely on past success, but past success cannot carry future growth. The world changes, and leadership must change with it. Leaders who continue to learn remain adaptable, resilient, and relevant. Their willingness to grow keeps the organization alive and dynamic. Their refusal to grow risks leaving it rigid and vulnerable.

Learning is not optional for leaders. It is a responsibility. It is the bridge that allows them to guide others with authenticity, relevance, and vision. By choosing to learn, leaders show that growth does not belong only to employees. It belongs to everyone, including those at the top. The strongest leaders are those who model the very culture they want to create: a culture where learning never stops.

True leadership is not proven in titles or strategies but in the daily choices that shape trust and connection. Every conversation, every response, and every decision is a chance to either reinforce walls or build bridges. The measure of a leader is found not in how much control they hold but in how much growth they inspire. The true legacy of leadership is not authority but the impact of the bridges built.

Chapter 11
Systems That Sustain Growth

Every leader teaches, whether they intend to or not. Teaching is not limited to classrooms or training sessions. It happens in the way a leader explains a decision, responds to mistakes, and models behavior. Employees are always learning, and much of what they learn comes from observing those in positions of authority. This means that leaders cannot escape the role of teacher. The only question is whether they will teach intentionally or accidentally.

When leaders teach intentionally, they see every interaction as a chance to build understanding and capability. They explain not only what to do but why it matters. They help employees see the connection between their work and the larger mission. They offer feedback that guides improvement rather than criticism that discourages. In doing so, they turn daily tasks into learning moments and transform ordinary workplaces into places of growth.

Accidental teaching happens when leaders underestimate their influence. A manager who cuts corners teaches that shortcuts are acceptable. A supervisor who reacts harshly to mistakes teaches that fear is the safest response. A director who avoids hard conversations teaches that silence is easier than honesty. These lessons are absorbed quickly, often more quickly than formal training because they are life experiences. If leaders are not careful, they may be teaching values they never intended to promote.

Teaching through leadership does not require formal lectures. It requires clarity, patience, and presence. A leader who takes the time to explain a decision teaches transparency. A leader who acknowledges an error teaches humility. A leader who asks for input teaches respect. These are lessons delivered not through manuals but through actions. They resonate because they are lived, not merely spoken.

One of the most effective ways leaders teach is by modeling curiosity. When a leader shows that they are eager to learn, employees recognize that growth is part of the culture. They see that questions are welcomed, that exploration is valued, and that improvement is continuous. This teaching by example is powerful because it shapes attitudes more deeply than words. People imitate what they observe more than what they are told, again because of life experiences.

Leaders also teach by shaping opportunities. When they delegate thoughtfully, they teach trust. When they challenge employees with new responsibilities, they teach confidence. When they provide guidance and support, they teach resilience. Every assignment becomes more than a task. It becomes a message about what the leader believes the employee is capable of. Leaders who treat delegation as teaching empower their teams to stretch beyond their current abilities.

The role of teacher also involves storytelling. Leaders who share their own journeys, including both successes and struggles, provide lessons that statistics and directives cannot. Stories humanize leadership. They reveal values, demonstrate perseverance, and connect abstract principles to real experiences. A story of how a leader overcame a challenge teaches more than instructions on how to avoid mistakes. It shows that growth is possible, even in the face of setbacks.

Being a teacher as a leader requires patience. People learn at different paces and in different ways. Some need repeated guidance, while others thrive with freedom. A leader who understands this does not treat teaching as a one-size-fits-all activity. They adapt their approach, and in turn they offer structure when needed and independence when appropriate. Patience in teaching is not indulgence. It is recognition that learning is a process, and growth takes time.

Leaders who resist the teaching role often miss opportunities to shape culture. They may see themselves only as decision-makers or task managers. But leadership without teaching leaves gaps. Employees may complete assignments, but they do not grow in understanding or capacity. They may follow directions, but they do not develop initiative. Without the teaching element of leadership, organizations stall because learning is limited to formal programs rather than embedded in daily work.

When leaders embrace their role as teachers, they multiply their influence. Each lesson, whether through words, actions, or attitudes, creates ripples. Those ripples shape not only current employees but also the next generation of leaders who learn from them. In this sense, leadership as teaching is a legacy. It extends beyond immediate results and into the future of the organization. Leaders who understand this leave behind more than accomplishments. They leave behind people who are wiser, stronger, and ready to build bridges of their own.

Chapter 12
Measuring and Sustaining Progress

A learning culture takes shape gradually. It grows from study, from conversations, from written reflection, and from analysis, all bound together by the consistency that gives it strength. Many organizations talk about learning as a value, but fewer live it in their routines. A true learning culture is not measured by the number of training programs offered. It is measured by whether people feel safe to ask questions, whether mistakes are treated as opportunities, whether curiosity is welcomed at every level, and whether growth is reflected in the way people perform in their work and in their lives.

The foundation of a learning culture is mindset. In organizations where knowledge is seen as fixed, people protect what they know instead of exploring what they do not. They see mistakes as threats rather than as steppingstones. This mindset creates walls that limit potential. A growth mindset does the opposite. It treats every challenge as a chance to expand, every question as a doorway, and every failure as a lesson. When this mindset is shared, learning becomes natural rather than forced.

Leaders play a central role in shaping this mindset. If they present themselves as finished products, employees will hide their own uncertainties. If they show curiosity, humility, and openness, employees will follow. Leaders who ask for feedback, who read and reflect, and who admit when they are still learning send a powerful message: growth is valued here. This example sets the tone for everyone else. When leaders stop learning, the culture stops with them.

A learning culture also depends on systems. It is not enough for individuals to be curious; the organization must create structures that support curiosity. This includes regular opportunities for development, spaces for collaboration, and processes for reflection. It also includes recognition for learning itself, not just for results. When people see that growth is noticed and valued, they continue to pursue it. When they see that only immediate outcomes are rewarded, they choose safety over exploration.

Feedback is one of the most important systems in a learning culture. In many organizations, feedback is rare, rushed, or uncomfortable. But when feedback is offered with respect and received with openness, it becomes a tool for collective improvement. A learning culture treats feedback not as criticism but as guidance. In this environment, walls of defensiveness fall, and bridges of trust and understanding rise.

Another key element is reflection. A culture that rushes from one task to the next without pause misses the lessons embedded in experience. Reflection can take many forms: team debriefs after projects, personal journaling, short huddles, or open conversations about what worked and what did not. These practices slow the pace just enough to turn action into insight. Without them, experience remains shallow. With them, even mistakes become valuable investments in the future.

Learning cultures also celebrate curiosity. Questions are welcomed, not seen as signs of ignorance. Employees are encouraged to explore beyond their immediate roles, to connect with colleagues in different areas, and to share what they discover. This exchange multiplies knowledge. It also strengthens relationships, as people realize they are not only workers but also learners together. A culture that celebrates curiosity is a culture that grows stronger with every interaction.

It is very important to comprehend that a learning culture is inclusive. It does not privilege certain voices or backgrounds. It recognizes that wisdom comes from many places and that everyone has something to contribute. When only a few are invited to learn or to teach, walls of hierarchy rise. When everyone is included, bridges of equity are built. The more voices are part of the learning process, the richer and more resilient the culture becomes.

The impact of a learning culture extends beyond the organization itself. It shapes how people approach their communities, their families, and their own personal growth. Employees who are encouraged to learn at work often bring that same curiosity into their lives. They become more adaptable, more reflective, and more connected. The influence ripples outward, proving that a culture of learning does not stop at the office. It becomes a way of living.

Building a learning culture requires patience. It does not happen overnight, and it is never complete. But each step matters. Each time a leader models curiosity, each time a team reflects honestly, and each time feedback is given with respect, the culture shifts. Over time, these shifts accumulate until learning is no longer an initiative or a program. It is simply the way things are done.

A learning culture ensures that growth never ends. It creates organizations that are resilient in the face of change, innovative in the face of challenges, and connected in the face of difference. More than that, it creates people who carry the spirit of learning wherever they go. And when that happens, the bridges built inside the organization extend far beyond it, shaping not just work but life itself.

Sustaining a learning culture also requires courage. New ideas can challenge traditions, and change can unsettle people who prefer certainty. Leaders and employees alike must be willing to step into the unknown, to try approaches that may not work, and to learn from results whether they succeed or fail. Courage in learning does not mean recklessness. It means choosing progress over comfort and growth over stagnation.

Ultimately, a learning culture is a promise to the future. It declares that the organization will not remain trapped in the patterns of the past but will continue to evolve. It assures employees that their potential is recognized and that their growth matters as much as their performance. And it demonstrates to the outside world that this is a place where people are not only valued for what they already know but also supported in becoming more than they imagined.

Chapter 13

Technology and Human Connection

Change often begins with simple conversations. A single exchange can spark curiosity, shift perspective, and open doors that once seemed closed. Conversations that open minds are not ordinary discussions. They are intentional, respectful, and shaped by the desire to understand rather than to win. They remind us that growth is achieved through dialogue that creates connection and not through argument.

At the heart of such conversations is the willingness to actively listen. People are more likely to open their minds when they feel heard. If a conversation becomes a competition of voices, defensiveness rises and curiosity fades. But when one person actively listens, asks thoughtful questions, and responds with patience, the other person feels safe enough to explore new possibilities. Active listening is the soil in which open-mindedness grows. Without it, even the best arguments fall on resistant ground.

Openness also depends on respect. Conversations that open minds are rooted in the recognition that every perspective has value. This does not mean that every perspective is equally effective, but it does mean that each one carries a story worth considering. Respect lowers walls and invites honesty. When people feel that their experiences are acknowledged, they are more likely to share openly. When they feel dismissed, they protect themselves by withdrawing or resisting. Respect transforms disagreement into dialogue and conflict into discovery.

Curiosity is another vital ingredient. Too often, conversations become opportunities to prove a point rather than to learn something new. Curiosity shifts the purpose. Instead of asking, *"How can I convince them?"* a curious person asks, *"What can I learn here?"* This change in attitude creates space for bridges to form. It turns conversations into opportunities for mutual growth rather than contests of who is right. Curiosity invites both people to step beyond the limits of their own perspective.

The environment of a conversation also matters. People are more likely to open their minds in spaces that feel safe and supportive. Leaders and colleagues can shape this environment by choosing words carefully, by controlling tone and body language, and very important, by ensuring that conversations are not rushed. A hurried exchange rarely produces openness. It may deliver decisions, but it does not deliver growth. When considerate time and attention are given, conversations expand beyond the surface and reach the heart of issues.

These principles apply not only to one-on-one dialogue but also to group discussions. In meetings, for example, conversations often default to efficiency. The goal is to finish quickly rather than to explore fully. Yet meetings can be powerful spaces for open minds if structured intentionally. This might mean asking each participant to share a perspective, pausing to reflect before moving on, or capturing questions rather than rushing to answers. Group conversations that encourage exploration rather than speed create bridges that connect people more deeply.

It is important to note that conversations that open minds do not always lead to agreement. Sometimes they lead to clarity about differences. But even that clarity is valuable. It prevents misunderstanding and reduces tension. When people walk away knowing they were heard, they are more willing to accept outcomes even if those outcomes do not match their preferences. Openness is not about achieving uniformity. It is about creating connection strong enough to handle diversity of thought.

Conversations that open minds also encourage self-reflection. As we listen to others, we inevitably examine our own assumptions. We notice where our beliefs come from, what experiences shaped them, and where they might be incomplete. In this way, dialogue becomes a mirror as well as a bridge. It shows us who we are while also showing us who we might become. Growth is not only external but internal, shaped by the willingness to let other voices inform our own.

Leaders carry the responsibility of creating these kinds of conversations. Their authority can either shut down dialogue or open it wider. When leaders encourage questions, invite debate, and reward honesty, they create a culture where open-minded conversations thrive. When they dismiss input or punish disagreement, they build walls that silence curiosity. Employees quickly recognize whether their contributions are truly welcome. Leaders who model openness show that growth is not only allowed but expected.

The power of conversations that open minds lies in their cumulative effect. A single open conversation can shift a moment. A pattern of open conversations can shift an entire culture. Over time, people begin to expect respect, curiosity, and active listening as the norm. They bring these qualities into their own interactions, multiplying the effect. Bridges spread, and walls crumble, one dialogue at a time.

Conversations that open minds remind us that growth is not imposed but invited. It happens not when one person demands change from another but when both step into dialogue with humility. In those moments, possibility expands. What once felt like a barrier becomes a path. And through these conversations, organizations and individuals alike discover that connection is not only possible but powerful.

The true measure of an open conversation is not whether it changes minds immediately but whether it leaves people willing to continue engaging. Sometimes the most meaningful shift is not agreement but a willingness to keep talking. When dialogue remains alive, growth remains possible. What closes the door is not difference but silence. As long as the conversation continues, the bridge holds.

Chapter 14
Resilient Organizations

Not every conversation begins in trust. Some begin with walls already built, whether from misunderstanding, conflict, or past disappointment. Dialogue that breaks walls is different from dialogue that opens minds. Its purpose is not to explore new ideas but to repair what has been damaged. It seeks to restore connection where it has been lost and to rebuild bridges that have collapsed. This kind of dialogue is harder, but it is also deeply necessary. Without it, walls grow thicker, and people drift farther apart.

Walls in communication rarely appear overnight. They are often the product of small moments that go unattended. A promise that was not kept, a concern that was ignored, or a disagreement that was handled poorly may not seem catastrophic at first. But when repeated, these moments stack like bricks until separation feels permanent. Dialogue that breaks walls begins by acknowledging the presence of the wall. Pretending it is not there does not make it disappear. In fact, denial often makes the wall stronger. Honesty, however difficult, is the first crack in its foundation.

Breaking walls requires vulnerability. Someone must take the first step to admit hurt, misunderstanding, or regret. This step may feel risky, but it signals courage and opens the door to reconciliation. When one person chooses honesty, it gives permission for the other to do the same. What begins as a single opening can widen into a pathway of understanding. Vulnerability does not weaken dialogue. It gives it strength, because it shows that trust is worth rebuilding.

Respect is equally important. When dialogue begins with blame, the wall grows taller. When it begins with respect, even in the presence of disagreement, the wall weakens. Respectful dialogue acknowledges the dignity of the other person regardless of past mistakes. It seeks not to erase conflict but to face it without contempt. In this way, respect turns confrontation into collaboration and defense into discovery.

Dialogue that breaks walls also requires patience. Repair does not happen in a single exchange. Trust that has been broken cannot be rebuilt overnight. People need time to test whether the change is real, to see whether words are followed by consistent actions. Every person must understand that progress will be gradual. Each respectful conversation is another stone removed from the wall. Over time, persistence creates enough space for bridges to be rebuilt.

Leaders often carry responsibility for initiating this kind of dialogue. Their position gives them the opportunity to set the tone. When they choose silence in the face of conflict, employees learn to remain silent as well. When they choose dialogue, employees learn that walls can be addressed rather than ignored. Leaders who admit mistakes, apologize when needed and invite honest conversation, send a powerful message that breaking walls is not only possible but expected.

Dialogue that breaks walls does not always lead to agreement, but it does lead to clarity. When people understand each other's perspectives, even if they do not agree, suspicion weakens. Transparency removes the shadows where mistrust thrives. Sometimes the wall does not crumble completely, but even small cracks create room for movement. That movement is enough to begin building a new foundation for trust.

The practice of breaking walls through dialogue strengthens the entire culture. It shows employees that conflict is not the end of connection but an opportunity to deepen it. It replaces the fear of disagreement with the confidence that reconciliation is possible. Over time, this confidence makes teams more resilient. They are no longer paralyzed by tension, because they know that walls can be addressed with honesty and care.

The most powerful outcome of dialogue that breaks walls is renewal. Relationships once thought damaged beyond repair can become stronger than before. When people walk through the process of addressing conflict openly and respectfully, they often emerge with deeper understanding and trust. The wall that once separated them becomes a reminder of what they overcame together. The experience itself becomes a bridge, one that can carry them forward with new strength.

Dialogue has the power to break walls because it touches the core of what it means to be human. We all want to be heard, respected, and valued. When dialogue provides these things, even in difficult circumstances, walls lose their hold. They may not disappear instantly, but they begin to crumble under the weight of honesty, respect, and persistence. With each word, each active listening moment, and each gesture of care and respect, the distance shortens. What once divided becomes a pathway for connection, and what once felt final becomes the beginning of renewal.

Chapter 15
Cultures That Last

Some conversations do more than exchange information or repair trust. They ignite movement. They awaken energy, stir motivation, and create clarity strong enough to push people forward. Conversations that inspire action are the bridge between vision and reality. Without them, even the best ideas remain abstract. With them, people find direction, courage, and commitment.

At their core, conversations that inspire action combine honesty with hope. They acknowledge reality without sugarcoating it, yet they point toward possibility. A leader who tells the truth about challenges while also painting a picture of what is possible creates credibility. Employees can trust the message because it is grounded in truth, and they can invest in it because it offers purpose. Inspiration is not born from exaggeration or empty promises. It is born from authenticity.

These conversations also draw on emotion. Facts and logic matter, but people are rarely moved to action by data alone. They act when they feel something. Leaders who share stories, personal experiences, or examples that connect emotionally reach people at a deeper level. Emotion does not replace reason, but it gives reason the energy to move. Without emotion, conversations may inform. With emotion, conversations transform.

Clarity is another vital quality. People cannot act on vague or confusing messages. Conversations that inspire action provide direction that is specific enough to be practical and broad enough to be meaningful. They answer the questions: *What do we need to do? Why does it matter? And how does each person contribute?* When these answers are clear, people no longer wonder where to focus their energy. They know, and they begin.

Conversations that inspire action also affirm identity. They remind people that they are capable, valued, and part of something greater. When employees hear not only what must be done but also why they matter in the process, they feel a sense of ownership. Ownership fuels commitment. It turns tasks into responsibilities and responsibilities into opportunities. When people believe they are essential to the mission, they give their best with energy rather than obligation.

The setting of these conversations matters too. They are most powerful when they are personal, whether one-on-one or in small groups, where individuals feel directly addressed. Large gatherings can also inspire, but the most lasting motivation often comes from personal exchanges where encouragement feels tailored. Leaders who make time for these conversations multiply their influence. Each person walks away with the sense that their contribution matters uniquely.

Inspiration must also be supported by consistency. A powerful conversation can spark motivation, but without follow-through, the spark disappears. Leaders must align their actions with their words, reinforce key messages, and celebrate progress along the way. Inspiration without reinforcement becomes disappointment. Inspiration with consistency becomes transformation. It creates momentum that continues long after the conversation ends.

Conversations that inspire action are not limited to leaders. Colleagues can inspire one another through encouragement, recognition, and belief. When teams learn to lift each other up, the culture becomes self-sustaining. Action is no longer driven solely by top-down communication but by shared commitment. Each voice carries the potential to ignite another, and the result is collective energy.

The ultimate power of these conversations is that they create movement toward something larger than individual goals. They remind people that their work contributes to a shared vision, whether it is serving a customer, improving a community, or shaping the future of the organization. When people see that their actions matter beyond themselves, they find meaning. And meaning is the most powerful fuel for sustained action.

Conversations that inspire action are bridges built with honesty, emotion, clarity, and consistency. They connect vision with commitment, possibility with effort, and individuals with collective purpose. They show us that words, when chosen with care and spoken with sincerity, have the power not only to inform but to transform. Through these conversations, leaders and teams together create momentum that carries growth forward. And when action is inspired through connection, progress does not just happen. It endures.

Chapter 16

A Future Without Walls

The vision of a future without walls is not naive optimism. It is the recognition that the barriers we often treat as permanent are, in truth, the result of choices we make. If walls are built through silence, fear, and division, then they can also be dismantled through honesty, courage, and connection. A future without walls is not a world free of difficulty. It is a world where difficulty is faced together, where trust is strong enough to carry people through conflict, and where communication replaces isolation.

When we imagine this kind of future, we see workplaces where people feel safe enough to share their ideas without hesitation. We see leaders who use authority not as a shield but as a platform to lift others. We see teams that value differences as sources of wisdom rather than as threats to stability. A future without walls is not about removing boundaries entirely. It is about creating connections strong enough that boundaries no longer become barriers.

This vision requires intention. Left alone, cultures drift toward self-protection. Walls are easier to build than bridges, because fear often feels safer than trust. But safety built on fear is fragile. It collapses at the first sign of pressure. Safety built on trust is resilient. It can withstand disagreement and difficulty because it rests on connection. A future without walls asks us to choose the harder, braver path of connection, again and again.

Each choice contributes to this future. Every time someone decides to actively listen rather than dismiss, they weaken a wall. Every time a leader chooses transparency over secrecy, they widen a bridge. Every time a team treats a mistake as an opportunity to learn rather than a reason to blame, they create new ground for growth. The future is not built in one dramatic moment. It is built in thousands of small acts of bridge-building that accumulate into lasting change.

A future without walls is not only possible. It is necessary. Organizations that continue to build walls will find themselves isolated, unable to adapt, and unable to inspire loyalty. They will also face higher turnover, as employees disengage and seek workplaces where they feel trusted and connected. Walls may hold people in place for a while, but they cannot hold their commitment. In contrast, organizations that build bridges will thrive, because they will carry within them the resilience, creativity, and trust needed to face whatever comes next. Growth is not guaranteed, but it is always possible when people choose to connect.

Chapter 17
The Cost of Walls, the Reward of Bridges

Walls are not free. They cost organizations in ways that are often hidden but always significant. They cost time, as people hesitate to speak, clarify, or collaborate. They cost talent, as employees disengage or leave because they do not feel valued. They cost trust, as relationships weaken under the weight of secrecy or defensiveness. The price of walls is high, even when it is not obvious.

Bridges, on the other hand, offer rewards that multiply. They save time, because open dialogue prevents confusion. They strengthen talent, because people feel invested and motivated. They build trust, because honesty becomes the norm. The reward of bridges is not only seen in efficiency or performance but also in the deeper loyalty and energy of people who know that their voices matter.

The contrast is clear when we look at organizations that rely on walls. They may appear strong on the outside, but inside, creativity slows, collaboration shrinks, and energy fades. Walls give an illusion of stability, but it is an illusion that cannot last. In moments of change or crisis, the cracks appear quickly. In contrast, organizations that invest in bridges remain flexible and resilient. They adapt because their people are engaged, committed, and connected.

At a personal level, the same is true. Walls built in relationships lead to distance and mistrust. Bridges built through respect and active listening lead to intimacy and strength. The cost of walls is disconnection. The reward of bridges is astonishing connection and productivity in life and at work. Each of us pays or receives the consequences of these choices every day.

The true question is not whether walls exist. They always will. The question is whether we are willing to pay their cost or whether we will choose the greater reward of building bridges. When we consider this choice honestly, the answer becomes clear. Walls may feel easier, but bridges always give more back than they take.

Walls also drain energy from leaders themselves. Managing distrust, conflict, and disengagement takes more effort than building connection. Leaders who rely on walls often find themselves exhausted, caught in a cycle of control rather than collaboration. In contrast, leaders who invest in bridges experience renewed energy because they are not carrying the burden alone. Shared trust lightens the load, and shared commitment multiplies results.

The ultimate reward of bridges is that they create cultures people do not want to leave. When employees feel valued, respected, and trusted, they bring not only their skills but also their hearts to the work. Loyalty is no longer forced; it grows naturally from the environment itself. Organizations that choose bridges build more than performance metrics. They build belonging. And belonging is the strongest foundation for growth that lasts.

Chapter 18

Growth That Never Stops

Growth is not a destination but a direction. It does not end when a certain goal is reached or when a milestone is celebrated. Growth is a continuous process of learning, adapting, and becoming more than we were yesterday. Cultures that embrace this truth never settle. They recognize that the moment growth stops, decline begins.

A culture of endless growth does not mean endless pressure. It does not demand constant expansion or unrealistic expectations. It means that curiosity, reflection, and improvement remain part of daily life. It means that people are encouraged to explore, to experiment, and to see every challenge as an opportunity. Growth that never stops is not about exhaustion. It is about renewal.

This kind of growth requires perspective. It asks us to view mistakes as teachers rather than enemies, to view diversity as strength rather than difficulty, and to view leadership as service rather than control. When people see growth this way, they stop fearing change and begin to embrace it. They realize that the end of one stage is the beginning of another, and that the process of becoming never truly ends.

The beauty of growth is that it spreads. A leader who continues to learn inspires employees to do the same. A team that reflects honestly on its work encourages other teams to reflect as well. An organization that values curiosity becomes known for innovation. The effect multiplies, shaping not only the culture but also the people within it. Growth that never stops creates individuals who carry the same spirit into every part of their lives.

In the end, growth is not measured only in results but in transformation. It is measured in the bridges built, the walls dismantled, and the people who become more open, more resilient, and more connected. This is the growth that never stops. It is not a goal to reach once and leave behind. It is a way of living, a way of leading, and a way of building a future where connection defines success.

Growth that never stops also requires balance. Without reflection, the push for growth can become pressure that wears people down rather than builds them up. True growth does not demand constant acceleration but invites renewal through cycles of action and pause, effort and rest. When individuals and organizations learn to honor these rhythms, growth becomes sustainable instead of exhausting.

This is why the most resilient cultures are not the loudest or the fastest. They are the ones that keep moving forward with steadiness, guided by curiosity and grounded in purpose. Their growth may not always make headlines, but it endures because it is built on consistency and connection.

Chapter 19

Beyond the Walls

I return to the image that has carried us from the beginning: bridges and walls. It is a simple metaphor, yet it captures the essence of how cultures grow or decline. Bridges represent connection, trust, and possibility. Walls represent division, fear, and limitation. Every culture, every leader, and every person chooses daily whether to build one or the other.

Going beyond the walls means recognizing that the barriers we face are not permanent. They are not unbreakable. They are the product of choices, of habits, of silence and fear. And if they are built by choice, they can also be dismantled by choice. To go beyond the walls is to decide that connection matters more than comfort, that growth matters more than control, and that trust matters more than power.

This book was not written to provide formulas or simple answers. It was written to remind us that connection is always possible, and that growth depends on it. The details will look different in every workplace, every community, and every relationship, but the truth remains constant: progress comes through bridges, not walls. The future belongs to those who choose to connect.

Going beyond the walls is not easy. It demands patience when frustration rises, humility when pride tempts us to defend, and courage when fear urges us to retreat. It asks us to be intentional in our words, consistent in our actions, and generous in our listening. These choices may seem small, but over time they become the difference between a culture that thrives and a culture that fractures.

If there is one truth I hope you carry forward, it is this: growth does not happens behind walls. It always happens on the bridges we choose to build. Each of us holds the power to shape that choice, in our conversations, in our leadership, and in the cultures we create. May you have the courage to go beyond the walls, to build bridges that last, and to discover that growth, when fueled by connection, never stops.